GW00320385

Classic
Essential

❧ ✿ ❧

BREAD
—AND—
BUNS

KÖNEMANN

∼ The Pleasures of Baking Bread ∼

Making bread can seem a daunting task to even the most experienced cook, an old-time chore filled with mysterious rituals and potential pitfalls. What if the yeast doesn't work? Won't it take all day to rise? Why bother when I can just go to the shop and buy bread? But when your kitchen is filled with the heady aroma of bread in the oven, when you cut the first slice and take a bite, you will know why you bothered. And with today's conveniences, such as thermostat-controlled ovens and reliable yeast, bread-making can be much easier than it was for bakers in the past.

For successful baking, it is important to understand how each step contributes to the finished product.

Dry Yeast: Dissolve dry yeast in warm water, sometimes with a little sugar to activate it. After about 5 minutes in a warm place, the mixture should be frothy and slightly increased in volume. If it isn't, discard it and start again. We used dried yeast in our recipes, as it is readily available from the supermarket, can be stored in the pantry, and carries a use-by date.

Fresh Yeast: Fresh compressed yeast may be substituted for dry yeast; 15 g of fresh yeast is equivalent to a 7 g sachet of dried. Fresh yeast is available from health food shops but is sometimes hard to obtain, and has quite a short storage life.

After yeast mixture has become frothy, it is added to the flour with any other ingredients.

Flour: The moisture content of flour can vary greatly between brands and even between batches. We have given a minimum and maximum amount of flour (e.g. 3–3 1/2 cups flour) to allow for this. Start with the minimum amount and add the remaining flour as necessary. Do not make the dough too dry—it will absorb more flour during kneading.

Kneading: This is an important step and determines the texture of the finished bread. Don't be tempted to give up after 5 minutes. The action is simple, and it is quite easy to get into a rhythm. Hold one end of the dough down with one hand, and stretch it away from you with the heel of the other hand. Fold the dough back together, make a quarter turn and repeat the action. When you have finished, gather dough into a ball; it should be smooth and elastic. For a soft, sticky dough, such as brioche, a dough scraper is used to gather the dough back together, while the other hand lifts the dough up in a stretch and slaps it back down onto the bench.

Proving: Place dough into a bowl, which has been lightly brushed with oil so that it won't stick, and cover loosely with lightly oiled plastic wrap or a clean, lightly floured cloth. Leave the bowl in a warm place (around 30°C is ideal) to allow dough to rise; this is called 'proving'. Do not put the dough in a very hot environment in an attempt to speed up the rising process: it will give an unpleasant flavour to the bread and may damage the yeast action. The dough will take longer to rise in a cooler environment, but with no adverse effect.

Left to right: coburg, free-form loaf with plait, plain white loaf and small wholemeal loaf.

When dough is ready it should be doubled in volume and not spring back when pressed with a fingertip.

'Punching Down': In this step the dough is knocked with the fist to expel the air. It is then lightly kneaded again for just one minute until smooth.

The dough is now ready to be shaped. This is illustrated in step-by-step pictures alongside some of the recipes. For best results, use strong heavy-duty baking trays for free-form loaves, and black bread tins for tinned loaves. The black surface contributes to an evenly browned crust.

Some of the fancier breads call for specific types of tins, which are available in department stores and specialty shops. We have suggested alternatives such as cake and loaf tins that you probably already have in your cupboard. Try to use tins close in size to the ones suggested, as this affects cooking times. Bread is usually proved one more time before baking.

Baking: Bake bread as directed in a preheated oven. At the end of cooking time, test for doneness by turning loaf out of tin and tapping the base with knuckles. Bread will sound hollow when cooked. If not, return to tin and bake for another 5–10 minutes. Remove from tin and cool on a wire rack.

Storage: Home-baked bread doesn't keep as long as commercial bread as it has no preservatives, and is best eaten on day of baking or toasted the next day. It keeps, tightly wrapped and frozen, for up to 3 months. Thaw at room temperature, and then 'refresh' in the oven for about 10 minutes.

~ Bread Loaves ~

Delicious bread is simple to make once you know how. These basic breads are an excellent starting point, as similar techniques are used in all bread making.

White Bread

Combine a 7 g sachet of dried yeast with 1/2 cup warm water in a small bowl; stir in 1 teaspoon caster sugar. Cover with plastic wrap; set aside for 5 minutes or until bubbles appear on the surface.

Sift 4 cups unbleached plain flour, 1 teaspoon salt, 2 tablespoons dried whole milk powder and 1 tablespoon caster sugar into a large bowl. Make a well in centre, add yeast, 1/4 cup cooking oil and 1 cup

warm water. Using hands or a large spoon, mix to a soft dough. Turn onto lightly floured surface; knead 10 minutes or until smooth and elastic. If needed, incorporate up to 1/2 cup of extra flour until dough is not sticky.

Place in a large, lightly oiled bowl. Leave, covered with a tea towel, in a warm place for 1 hour or until well risen. Punch dough down and knead for 1 minute.

Divide and shape into loaves or rolls. Leave, covered with plastic

wrap, for 45 minutes or until well risen. Place in a tin which has been brushed lightly with melted butter or oil. Or mould into free-form shapes and place on a greased baking tray.

Bake in tins in a 210°C (Gas 190°C) over for 10 minutes; lower heat to 180°C, bake an extra 30–40 minutes. Bake free-form loaves in a 210°C (Gas 190°C) oven for 10 minutes; lower heat to 180°C and cook for 20–30 minutes. Cooking times will

vary depending upon size of loaves or rolls. To test for doneness, tap bottom of bread with knuckles; a hollow sound indicates bread is cooked. Or skewer through base of bread; bread is cooked when skewer comes out clean. **Note** Dough is enough for 1 large, 2 medium or 3 small loaves; or 16–24 rolls.

Wholemeal Bread
Replace plain white flour with plain wholemeal flour and follow the recipe for white bread. For a lighter bread, use half plain flour and half wholemeal flour.

Free-form Loaves
Coburg: This crusty round loaf has one or more cuts on top, often in the shape of a cross, made just before loaves are placed in the oven.
Cob: A variation of Coburg, a plain crusty, round loaf with no cuts on the top.

Oval shaped loaves are another alternative. Decorate with cuts or toppings of your choice.

Clockwise from bottom left: wholemeal coburg, white free-form loaf with plait, small wholemeal, herbed tinned loaf, plain white, white coburg with criss cross pattern, wholemeal free-form oval loaf.

Herbed Tinned Loaf
For a creative alternative to a white loaf, roll the dough to a 20 x 30 cm rectangle. Sprinkle with chopped fresh herbs and finely chopped sun-dried tomatoes. Roll as for a swiss roll and place in tin with seam side down. Cook as for white bread.

～ Rolls ～

Create your own selection of delicious bread rolls using plain or wholemeal bread dough, and the toppings and glazes from pages 8–9.

Parker House

Roll out dough for white or brown bread to 1 cm thick. Cut out rounds with 8 cm plain floured cutter. Crease across the rounds slightly off-centre with the back edge of a

From left to right by row: spiral and knot rolls; free-form flat round rolls; herb dough variation of poppy, oval rolls and poppies; free-form herb rolls; clover leaf rolls; sliced dinner roll and crescents; filled dinner rolls.

knife. Fold at crease, and then press down lightly. Place 5 cm apart on lightly oiled trays. Cover and set aside in a warm place for 20 minutes or until dough is well risen. Brush with glaze of your choice. Bake in 180°C oven for 15–20 minutes. See illustration page 8.

Crescent Rolls

Use half of the prepared white or wholemeal bread dough. Heat 1 tablespoon oil in frying pan; lightly fry 1 finely chopped onion, 2 slices finely chopped bacon

and 2 teaspoons chopped fresh rosemary; cool. Divide dough in half. Roll each portion into a 30 cm circle. Spread circles with a thin layer of tomato paste, and then with onion mixture. Cut each circle into 12 wedges; starting at wide end, roll each wedge into a crescent. Place 5 cm apart on lightly oiled tray. Leave, covered, in a warm place for 20 minutes or until well risen. Brush with whole egg and water glaze. Bake in 180°C oven for 15–20 minutes.

Spiral Rolls

Divide bread dough into 16–24 even pieces. Roll each piece into a 30 cm long rope. Shape into tight spirals, tuck under ends; seal. Place 5 cm apart on lightly oiled trays. Cover with plastic wrap; leave in a warm place for 20 minutes or until well risen. Brush with glaze or topping of choice. Bake in 180°C oven for 15–20 minutes.

Knot Rolls

Divide bread dough into 16–24 even pieces. Roll into 30 cm long ropes. Tie each rope in a loose knot. Place 5 cm apart on lightly oiled trays. Proceed as in Spiral Rolls.

Oval Rolls

Divide bread dough into 16–24 even pieces, and then shape into ovals. Leave plain or slash tops once lengthways, or twice diagonally. Place 5 cm apart on lightly oiled trays. Proceed as for Spiral Rolls.

Filled Dinner Rolls

Divide bread dough into 16–24 even pieces. Form into rounds; roll to 10 cm circles. Place a teaspoon of filling in circle centres. Enclose with the dough, pinching the seams underneath. Place, seam downwards, 5 cm apart, on lightly oiled trays. Proceed as for Spiral Rolls.

Clover Leaf Rolls

Divide bread dough into 16–24 even pieces. Divide each piece into 3 even-sized balls; place the trio of balls from each piece close together on lightly oiled trays, with 5 cm between each trio. Proceed as for Spiral Rolls.

Poppies

Divide bread dough into 16–24 even-sized rounds, and then use your hands to flatten them slightly. Using scissors, snip five evenly spaced 2 cm cuts into edge of each roll. Place 5 cm apart on lightly oiled trays. Proceed as for Spiral Rolls.

~ Toppings, Glazes & Flavourings ~

Create your own specialty breads and rolls with these delicious variations—from
a delicate, light sheen through to a cheese and herb flavouring.

Toppings

Before baking, sprinkle
dough with flour, rolled
oats, crushed rock salt,
cracked wheat or grated
Cheddar. Or try seeds
such as poppy, sesame,
caraway, pumpkin, dill,
fennel or sunflower.

Spread 1 tablespoon
tomato paste combined
with 2 tablespoons olive
oil on dough. Top with
dried thyme or rosemary.

Glazes/washes

To use before baking:
Deep crust colour:
Beat a whole egg with
1 teaspoon water.

Very deep colour:
Beat 1 egg yolk with
1 teaspoon water.
*Rich, dark gleam on
savoury breads:*
Beat 1 egg with
1 teaspoon oil, salt
and pepper.
Crisp crust: Whisk
together 1 egg white
with 1 teaspoon water.
Light sheen: Brush with
milk or melted butter.
To use after baking:
Soft crust: Remove loaf
from oven, brush with
melted butter. Return to
oven for 2 minutes.
Remove, brush with
butter; cool.

Glossy crust: Whisk
1 egg white with
1 tablespoon water.
Brush cooked, hot
bread with glaze, then
return to the oven
for 5 minutes; cool.
Sweet, glossy crust:
Combine 1 tablespoon
sugar with 2 tablespoons
milk. Brush on hot
bread. Return to oven
for 5 minutes; cool.
Sugar Glaze:
Dissolve 1/4 cup sugar
in 2 tablespoons water
over low heat. Boil
for 2 minutes until
mixture is syrupy, then
brush on hot bread.

Gelatine Glaze: Mix
1 tablespoon water,
1 teaspoon sugar and
1 teaspoon gelatine
in small bowl. Dissolve
over a pan of simmering
water. Brush on hot bread.
Honey Glaze: Brush
warm honey on hot
bread. Repeat 2–3 times.
Apricot Glaze: Combine
1/2 cup sieved apricot
jam with 2 teaspoons
of warmed brandy.
Brush on hot bread
several times.

Flavourings

Mix into dough, or brush
rolled dough with melted
butter, spread with
flavouring and roll up.
Mixed Herbs: Combine
2–3 tablespoons of
chopped fresh herbs or a
teaspoon each of dried
thyme and rosemary,
and 1–2 cloves crushed
garlic (optional).
Seeds: Add 2–3 table-
spoons dried caraway,
fennel, dill or aniseed.
Cheese and Herb: Add
1 cup grated Cheddar,
1/2 cup grated Parmesan,
1/4 teaspoon garlic
powder, 2 tablespoons
chopped fresh parsley,
and 1/2 teaspoon each of
dried thyme, oregano
and marjoram.
Olive: Add 1–2 cups
chopped pitted or stuffed
green olives, or finely
chopped black olives,
with 2 tablespoons
chopped fresh herbs.
Onion and bacon: Cook
1 large finely chopped
onion and 2 finely
chopped bacon rashers
in a tablespoon of oil;
cool. Add 2 tablespoons
chopped fresh chives.

*From left to right by row:
knot and clover leaf rolls
with egg white and water
glaze; oval and spiral
rolls with egg white
glaze; free-form herb
rolls with egg yolk and
water glaze; Parker
House rolls with egg and
water glaze; three rows
of buns with assorted
toppings and glazes;
filled dinner rolls with
egg yolk glaze and seeds.*

Nuts: Add 2 cups whole
or chopped nuts: roasted
almonds, pecans, walnuts.
*Sun-dried tomatoes or
capsicum:* Add 1/2 cup
drained, chopped sun-
dried tomatoes or
capsicum, 4 finely
chopped spring onions,
and 2 tablespoons
chopped fresh herbs.

∽ Sourdough Rye Bread ∽

Preparation time:
**40 minutes +
1½ hours rising +
1–3 days standing**
Total cooking time:
40 minutes

Makes 2 loaves

Sourdough Starter
**7 g sachet dried yeast
1 teaspoon caster sugar
2 cups rye flour
1¾ cups warm water**

Bread Dough
**1 cup rye flour
3½–4½ cups unbleached
  plain flour**

**¼ cup soft brown
  sugar
3 teaspoons caraway
  seeds
2 teaspoons salt
7 g sachet dried
  yeast, extra
1 cup warm water,
  extra
¼ cup oil**

**1·∽To make
sourdough starter:**
Combine yeast, sugar,
rye flour and warm
water in a medium bowl.
Cover with plastic wrap
and set aside overnight
at room temperature to
sour. For a stronger sour
flavour, leave aside for
up to 3 days.
**2·∽To make bread
dough:** Brush a large
baking tray with oil or
melted butter. In a large
bowl, combine rye flour,
3½ cups of plain flour,
sugar, seeds and salt.
Dissolve yeast in warm
water. Make a well in
the centre of the flour
mixture; add sourdough
starter, dissolved yeast

and oil. Mix, using a
wooden spoon, then
hands, until dough forms
a rough, slightly sticky
ball which leaves the
side of the bowl. Add
extra flour, if necessary.
3·∽Turn onto a lightly
floured surface. Knead
for 10 minutes or until
smooth and elastic.
Incorporate any of the
remaining flour, if
needed. Place dough in
large, lightly oiled bowl.
Leave, covered with
plastic wrap, in a warm
place for 45 minutes or
until the dough is well
risen. Punch dough
down, and then knead
for 1 minute. Divide

dough into 2 even-sized
portions. Shape into
round or oblong loaves;
place on tray. Sprinkle
with rye flour; use end
of wooden spoon handle
to punch holes 2 cm
deep in top, or slash
3 cuts in top. Leave,
covered with plastic
wrap, in warm place for
45 minutes or until
dough is well risen.
Sprinkle with extra
flour. Bake in preheated
180°C oven 40 minutes
or until skewer inserted
in centre comes out clean.
Cool on a wire rack.
Serve with cheese and
gherkins, if desired.
Note·∽If a large tray is
not available, cook the
loaves separately. Leave
one half to rise again
while cooking first loaf.
This bread may also be
cooked in tins.
  Bread will keep
well for up to 5 days in
an airtight container.

Make a well in the centre of flour mixture, and then add the sourdough starter.

Shape dough into round or oblong loaves and place on prepared tray.

∼ Focaccia ∼

Preparation time:
**50 minutes + 1 hour
50 minutes standing**
Total cooking time:
25 minutes

Makes 1 flat loaf

7 g sachet dried yeast	**Topping**
1 cup warm water	1 tablespoon olive oil
1 teaspoon caster sugar	1–2 cloves garlic, crushed
2 tablespoons olive oil	12 black olives
3–3¼ cups unbleached plain flour	fresh rosemary sprigs
1 tablespoon full cream milk powder	1 teaspoon dried oregano
½ teaspoon salt	1–2 teaspoons coarse sea salt

1. Brush a 28 x 18 cm rectangular tin with oil or melted butter. Combine yeast, water and sugar in a large bowl and stir to dissolve the yeast. Cover with plastic wrap and leave in a warm place for about 10 minutes or until frothy; add the oil. Sift 3 cups of the flour, milk powder and salt onto the yeast mixture. Beat with a wooden spoon until the mixture is well combined. Add enough of the reserved flour to form a soft dough, and then turn onto a lightly floured surface.

2. Knead 10 minutes or until dough is smooth and elastic. Place dough in a large, lightly oiled bowl; brush surface of dough with oil. Cover with plastic wrap and leave in a warm place for 1 hour or until well risen. Punch down dough and knead for 1 minute. Roll into a rectangle, 28 x 18 cm, and place in prepared tin. Cover with plastic wrap and leave to rise in a warm place for 20 minutes. Using the handle of a wooden spoon, press dough all over at regular intervals to form indents 1 cm deep. Cover with plastic wrap and set aside for 30 minutes or until dough is well risen.

3. **To make Topping:** Brush combined olive oil and garlic over surface. Top with olives and rosemary sprigs; sprinkle with oregano and salt.

4. Preheat oven to 180°C. Bake 20–25 minutes or until golden and crisp. Cut into large squares and serve warm.

Note Best eaten on the day of baking. May be reheated.

Stand yeast mixture in a warm place for 10 minutes or until frothy.

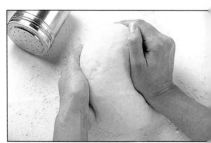

Knead dough for 10 minutes or until smooth and elastic.

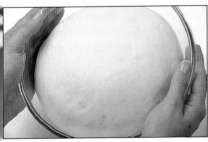

*Stand dough in oiled mixing bowl for
1 hour or until dough is well risen.*

*Using the tip of a wooden spoon handle,
make regular indents in dough.*

∼ French Bread Loaf ∼

Preparation time:
**35 minutes + 1 hour
40 minutes standing**
Total cooking time:
30 minutes

Makes 1 large loaf

**2¼–2½ cups
unbleached plain
flour**
**¼ cup unbleached
wholemeal flour**
1 teaspoon salt
7 g sachet dried yeast
1 cup warm water
1 egg white
**1 tablespoon water,
extra**

---

1 ∼ Brush a large, long baking tray or a bread stick pan with melted butter or oil. Sift 2¼ cups of the plain flour together with the wholemeal flour and salt into a large bowl, and then make a well in the centre of the flour. Dissolve the yeast in the warm water and add to flour. Using a wooden spoon, mix the dough into a rough, slightly sticky ball.
2 ∼ Turn onto a lightly floured surface and knead for 10 minutes or

until the dough is smooth and elastic. Incorporate some of the remaining flour, if necessary. Place dough in a large, lightly oiled bowl and brush surface of dough with oil. Cover and set aside in a warm place for 1 hour or until the dough is well risen.
3 ∼ Punch down dough and knead for 1 minute. Flatten or roll dough into a 45 cm x 18 cm rectangle. Roll up firmly into a long sausage shape. Taper ends, and then place the dough diagonally on prepared tray, or in a bread stick pan. Cover with plastic wrap and set aside in a warm place for about 40 minutes or until the dough is well risen.
4 ∼ Preheat oven to 210°C (Gas 190°C). Pour 2 cups of hot water into a shallow baking dish and place on bottom of oven (this helps to make a crisp crust). Brush loaf with combined lightly beaten egg white and water. Slash loaf diagonally with a sharp knife or razor at regular intervals about 5 cm apart. Bake in the preheated oven for 15 minutes. Lower the

oven temperature to 180°C. Quickly brush loaf again with glaze, and bake for a further 15 minutes or until cooked. Remove from tray or pan and cool on a wire rack. Serve with soft cheeses, such as Camembert or Brie or just plain with butter. Delicious also served as an accompaniment to salads, soups and pasta dishes.
Note ∼ This French bread stick is best if eaten on the day of baking. It also freezes very well, and is good to have on hand for quick snacks.

You may prefer to make 6–8 individual rolls. To do this, roll dough into required shapes and bake for 10 minutes at 180°C. Lower the temperature to 160°C and bake rolls for 10 minutes further or until cooked.

Bread stick pans are available from specialty kitchenware shops.

Using a wooden spoon, mix flour mixture and dissolved yeast into a sticky ball.

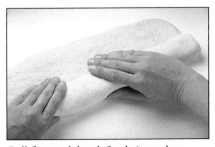

Roll flattened dough firmly into a long sausage shape.

~ Traditional Corn Bread ~

Preparation time:
15 minutes
Total cooking time:
25 minutes

Makes one 20 cm loaf

1 cup cornmeal	¹/₂ teaspoon bicarbonate
2 tablespoons caster	of soda
sugar	¹/₂ teaspoon salt
1 cup plain flour	1 egg, lightly beaten
2 teaspoons baking	1 cup buttermilk
powder	60 g butter, melted

1~Preheat oven to 210°C (Gas 190°C). Brush a 20 cm square cake tin with oil or melted butter, and line the base with baking paper. Place the cornmeal and sugar in a large bowl. Add the sifted flour, baking powder, soda and salt and mix thoroughly.

2~Combine beaten egg, buttermilk and melted butter in a large jug. Stir mixture quickly into dry ingredients. Stir only until ingredients are moistened.

3~Pour mixture into prepared tin and smooth surface. Bake for 20–25 minutes or until skewer inserted in centre comes out clean. Place on wire rack and leave to cool for 10 minutes before turning out. Cut into squares and serve while warm with butter and cheese.

Note~Best eaten on day of baking. For successful results use fine to medium cornmeal which is available at most health food stores.

~ Beer Bread ~

Preparation time:
10 minutes
Total cooking time:
40 minutes

Makes 1 loaf

3¹/₄ cups plain flour	50 g butter, cubed
3 teaspoons baking	375 ml can beer
powder	¹/₄ cup plain flour,
1 teaspoon salt	extra
1 tablespoon caster	dill seeds, extra
sugar	coarse sea salt
2 teaspoons dill seeds	

1~Preheat oven to 210°C (Gas 190°C). Brush a baking tray with melted butter or oil. Sift flour, baking powder and salt into a large bowl. Add sugar and seeds; stir to combine.

Use your fingers to rub butter cubes into the mixture. Make a well in the centre and pour in beer all at once. Using a wooden spoon, quickly mix to a soft dough.

2~Turn out onto floured surface; sprinkle extra flour onto hands and dough. Knead for 1–2 minutes until dough forms a smooth ball. Elongate ball slightly, flatten a little, and with the blunt end of a large

Traditional Corn Bread (top right) and Beer Bread

knife press down 2 cm along centre. Brush surface with water, and then sprinkle liberally with extra dill seeds and coarse salt.

3. Bake 20 minutes; lower temperature to 180°C and bake for 15–20 minutes or until cooked. Test for doneness by tapping base with knuckles. A hollow sound indicates bread is cooked. Remove from oven; place on a wire rack and leave to cool.

Note Best eaten on day of cooking. Also freezes well.

~ Potato Bread ~

Preparation time:
45 minutes + 1³/₄ hours standing
Total cooking time:
40 minutes

Makes one 25 cm loaf

---

7 g sachet dried yeast
¹/₄ cup warm water
3¹/₂–4 cups unbleached plain flour
1 teaspoon salt
2 tablespoons full cream milk powder
1 cup warm cooked mashed potato

¹/₂ cup chopped fresh chives
1 cup warm water, extra
1 egg white, to glaze
2 teaspoons cold water
sunflower or pepita seeds

---

1. Brush a 25 cm round cake tin with melted butter or oil. Line base with baking paper. Dissolve yeast in warm water, cover; leave in a warm place 5 minutes or until frothy. Sift 3¹/₂ cups of the flour, salt and milk powder into a large bowl. Using a fork, mix potato and chives through flour mixture. Add the yeast mixture and extra warm water; mix until combined. Add enough of the remaining flour to make a soft dough.

2. Turn onto a lightly floured surface. Knead for 10 minutes or until dough is smooth and elastic. Place in an oiled bowl; brush surface of dough with oil. Cover with plastic wrap; set aside in warm place for 1 hour or until well risen. Punch down dough; knead for 1 minute. Divide into 12 equal pieces. Form each piece into a smooth ball.

3. Place 2 layers of 6 evenly spaced balls in a daisy pattern in tin. Cover with plastic wrap; leave to rise 45 minutes or until dough has risen to top of tin. Brush with combined egg white and water; sprinkle seeds onto the centre ball.

4. Preheat oven to 210° C (Gas 190°C); bake for 15 minutes. Reduce oven to 180°C; bake 20 minutes or until skewer inserted in centre comes out clean. Leave for 10 minutes; turn out on a wire rack to cool. Serve with herb butter.

Note Depending on moisture content of potato, extra flour may have to be added to make a soft, slightly sticky dough. Keeps for up to 3 days in an airtight container.

Using a fork, mix the potato and chives through the flour mixture.

Punch down dough and then knead for 1 minute.

Place 2 layers of 6 balls each in a daisy pattern in prepared tin.

Sprinkle sunflower seeds onto the centre ball in the daisy pattern.

～ Pumpernickel ～

Preparation time:
1 hour + 2¹/₄ hours standing
Total cooking time:
50 minutes

Makes 2 loaves

2 x 7 g sachets dried
  yeast
¹/₂ cup warm water
1 teaspoon caster sugar
2 cups cold water
¹/₄ cup molasses
¹/₄ cup cider vinegar
90 g butter
30 g dark chocolate,
  chopped
1 tablespoon instant
  coffee

3¹/₂–4¹/₂ cups
  unbleached plain flour
3 cups rye flour
1 cup bran
1 tablespoon caraway
  seeds
2 teaspoons fennel seeds
1 teaspoon salt
1 egg white
1 tablespoon water,
  extra
caraway seeds, extra

1. Brush a 20 cm round cake tin and a 28 x 12 cm loaf or bread tin with oil (see Note). Line the bases of the tins with baking paper. Dissolve yeast in warm water and add the sugar. Cover with plastic wrap and leave in a warm place for 5 minutes or until mixture is frothy. Heat cold water, molasses, vinegar, butter, dark chocolate and coffee in a medium pan until mixture is just warmed and butter and chocolate have melted.

2. Combine 3¹/₂ cups of the plain flour, rye flour, bran, caraway and fennel seeds and salt in a large bowl. Make a well in the centre; pour yeast and warmed chocolate mixture into the flour. Using a wooden spoon, then hands, combine dough until it leaves the side of the bowl and forms a firm, sticky ball.

3. Turn out onto a heavily floured surface and knead 10 minutes. Incorporate sufficient remaining plain flour to make a dense but smooth and elastic dough. Divide in half; place in 2 lightly oiled bowls. Brush surface of dough with melted butter or oil. Cover with plastic wrap and leave in a warm place 1¹/₄ hours or until well risen. Punch down doughs and knead each one for 1 minute. Shape into 2 loaves and place into prepared tins. Cover with lightly oiled plastic wrap and leave in a warm place 1 hour or until well risen.

4. Preheat oven to 180°C. Glaze dough with combined egg white and water and sprinkle with seeds.

Bake for 50 minutes or until well browned. During last 15 minutes, cover loaves with foil to prevent excess browning. Leave in tins 15 minutes before turning out onto a wire rack to cool. Serve with soft cheeses, olives, smoked salmon and dill pickles.

Note. Any shape of 7–cup capacity tin is suitable for this recipe.

Will keep for up to one week in an airtight container.

Add the yeast and warmed chocolate mixture to flour.

Turn out onto a heavily floured surface and knead for 10 minutes.

∼ Damper ∼

Preparation time:
10 minutes
Total cooking time:
35–40 minutes

3 cups self-raising flour 1 cup wholemeal self- raising flour	1 teaspoon salt 1¹/₂–1³/₄ cups milk 30 g butter, melted

Makes 1 round loaf

1∼Preheat oven to 210°C (190°C Gas). Brush a baking tray with melted butter or oil. Sift flours and salt into a large bowl and return any husks to mixture; make a well in the centre of the flour.
2∼Combine milk and butter and pour 1¹/₂ cups of the liquid onto the flour. Using a knife, mix quickly and lightly in a cutting motion. Add remaining milk if the mixture is too dry. The mixture will leave the side of the bowl and form a rough, slightly sticky ball.
3∼Turn out onto a lightly floured surface; knead 1 minute until dough forms a soft, smooth 18-cm ball. Place on prepared tray; flatten slightly. With a sharp knife, cut 2 slits 2 cm deep across dough to form a cross. Brush top with extra milk and sprinkle with a little extra wholemeal flour.
4∼Bake 15 minutes, then reduce temperature to 180°C and cook for a further 20–25 minutes or until damper is golden brown and cooked. The base will sound hollow when tapped. Cool on a wire rack. To serve, slice or pull apart and butter. Spread with jam, if desired.
Note∼Best eaten on day of baking.

Use all white flour for a lighter damper, or use half wholemeal and half white for a heavier one.

∼ Onion Bread ∼

Preparation time:
10 minutes
Total cooking time:
1 hour 20 minutes

2 tablespoons olive oil
2 onions, thinly sliced
3 cups self-raising flour
35 g sachet dried French
  onion soup mix
	2 cups buttermilk
	¹/₄ cup self-raising
	  flour, extra
	milk, to glaze

Makes 1 loaf

1∼Brush a large baking tray with oil. Preheat oven to 180°C. Heat oil in a large frying pan, add the onion and cook, stirring frequently, over low heat for 20 minutes or until onion is very soft and lightly browned. Drain on paper towels, and then cool.
2∼In a large bowl, combine sifted flour, soup mix and half the cooked onion, stir; make a well in the centre.
3∼Add buttermilk all at once; stir quickly to

Damper (top) and Onion Bread

form a soft, sticky dough. Turn out onto floured surface and flour hands and surface of dough. Gently and quickly incorporate enough of the extra flour to form a smooth ball. **4** Place on tray and shape into an elongated loaf. Use scissors to snip surface of loaf at 3 cm intervals; brush with milk. Place in oven and bake for 45 minutes. Remove from oven and scatter remaining onion over surface. Return to oven and bake a further 10–15 minutes or until bread sounds hollow when tapped on base. Remove and place on wire rack to cool. **Note** Best eaten on the day of baking. Reheats well.

～ Rosettas ～

Preparation time:
40 minutes + 2 hours standing
Total cooking time:
25 minutes

Makes 10

7 g sachet dried yeast	1¹/₄ cups warm water, extra
2 tablespoons warm water	4¹/₄ –4¹/₂ cups unbleached plain flour, sifted
50 g butter, softened	1 teaspoon salt
¹/₄ cup olive oil	milk, to glaze
¹/₄ cup caster sugar	

1～Brush a large baking tray with melted butter or oil. Dissolve yeast in warm water in a small bowl. Cover with plastic wrap; set aside 5 minutes or until frothy. Place yeast mixture, butter, oil, sugar and extra water in a large bowl; stir to combine.
2～Add 4¹/₄ cups of sifted flour and salt to yeast mixture. Using a wooden spoon, stir to combine. Dough will leave side of bowl and form a rough, sticky ball. Turn out onto floured surface. Knead 10 minutes or until dough is smooth and elastic. If necessary, add remaining flour to make a smooth dough. Place dough in a large, lightly oiled bowl; brush surface of dough with melted butter or oil. Cover with plastic wrap and leave in a warm place for 1 hour or until well risen.
3～Punch dough down; knead 1 minute. Divide into 10 even portions. Shape each piece into a smooth ball; place 5 cm apart on prepared trays. Using a 3 cm round cutter, press a 1 cm deep indent into centre of each ball. With a sharp knife or razor, slash 5 evenly-spaced, 1 cm deep cuts down the side of each roll. Cover with plastic wrap; leave in a warm place for 1 hour or until well risen.
4～Preheat oven to 180°C. Brush rolls with milk and sift a fine layer of plain flour over top. Bake for 25 minutes or until cooked. Cool on a wire rack.
Note～If large tray is not available, cook in two batches. Let half of the dough rise while one batch cooks.

Best eaten on day of cooking. May be frozen for up to 1 month.

Brush surface of dough with melted butter or oil.

Using a round cutter, press an indent into the centre of each roll.

Slash evenly-spaced cuts down the side of each roll.

Sift a fine layer of plain flour over top of uncooked rosettas.

～ Grissini ～

Preparation time:
**40 minutes +
20 minutes standing**
Total cooking time:
25 minutes

Makes 18

---

7 g sachet dried yeast
1/2 cup warm water
2/3 cup milk
50 g butter
1 tablespoon caster
  sugar
31/2–4 cups
  unbleached plain
  flour
1 teaspoon salt
rock salt, sesame or
  poppy seeds, to coat

1～Brush 3 baking trays with melted butter or oil. Dissolve yeast in warm water in a small bowl. Cover with plastic wrap, then leave in a warm place for 5 minutes or until frothy. In a small pan heat the milk, butter and sugar until the mixture is just warm and the butter is melted.

2～Place 3 1/2 cups of the flour and the salt in a large bowl. Add yeast and milk mixture and mix thoroughly until well combined. Add enough of the remaining flour to make a soft dough. Turn onto a lightly floured surface and knead for 10 minutes or until the dough is smooth and elastic. Divide the dough into 18 even-sized pieces.

3～Roll each piece to the thickness of a pencil and about 30 cm in length. Preheat oven to 210°C (Gas 190°C). Place pieces 3 cm apart on baking trays. Cover with plastic wrap and leave for 20 minutes.

4～Brush dough with cold water and sprinkle with rock salt or seeds. Bake for 15–20 minutes or until golden brown. Remove from oven and cool on a wire rack. Reduce oven to 180°C. Return grissini to trays, and bake for 5–10 minutes or until they are dried out and crisp. Delicious with soups, salads, dips and pre-dinner drinks.

Note～Grissini will keep well for up to 1 week in an airtight container, and also freezes well.

Heat milk, butter and sugar until mixture is just warm and butter is melted.

Turn dough out of mixing bowl onto a lightly floured surface.

Roll dough to the thickness of a pencil and a length of around 30 cm.

Sprinkle uncooked grissini with rock salt, or sesame or poppy seeds.

～ Italian Bread ～

Preparation time:
**30 minutes +
2 hours standing**
Total cooking time:
40 minutes

Makes 1 loaf

cornmeal	1 tablespoon olive oil
7 g sachet dried yeast	1 cup warm water, extra
$1/4$ cup warm water	cornmeal or flour, extra
3–$3^1/2$ cups unbleached plain flour	
1 teaspoon salt	*Glaze*
1 tablespoon honey	1 tablespoon water
	$1/2$ teaspoon salt

1～Sprinkle a baking tray with cornmeal. Dissolve yeast in warm water. Cover with plastic wrap; leave in a warm place 5 minutes or until frothy. Sift 3 cups of flour with salt into a large bowl; make a well in the centre. Pour in yeast, honey, oil and extra water. Using a wooden spoon, stir until mixture is well combined and forms a rough ball. Turn out onto a floured surface and knead for 10 minutes or until the dough is smooth and elastic. Add remaining flour as necessary to form a smooth dough.

2～Place dough in a large, lightly oiled bowl. Brush surface of dough with oil. Cover and leave in a warm place for 1 hour or until well risen. Punch down dough and knead for 1 minute.

3～Shape dough into a smooth 18 cm ball, place on prepared tray and flatten top. Using a sharp knife or razor, slash top of dough with 1 cm deep cuts at 3 cm intervals in a criss-cross pattern. Cover and leave in warm place for 1 hour or until well risen.

4～Preheat oven to 180°C. Place a shallow baking dish containing 2 cups water in bottom of oven. (This helps form a hard crust on bread.) Brush dough with glaze of combined water and salt; sprinkle with cornmeal or flour. Bake 35–40 minutes or until base sounds hollow when tapped. Cool on a wire rack. Spread with ricotta and serve with prosciutto and sun-dried tomatoes, if desired.
Note～Best on day of baking. Reheats well.
The top of the dough may be slashed with a wide circle, if preferred.

Prepare baking tray by sprinkling it evenly with cornmeal.

Punch down risen dough and then knead for 1 minute.

Using a sharp knife or razor, slash surface of dough in a criss-cross pattern.

Sprinkle surface of uncooked dough lightly with cornmeal or flour.

～ Oatmeal Bread ～

Preparation time:
**45 minutes + 1³/₄ hours
standing**
Total cooking time:
45 minutes

Makes 1 loaf

1 cup rolled oats	¹/₂ cup warm milk
1¹/₂ cups water	1 tablespoon soft brown
2 x 7 g sachets dried	sugar
yeast	1 teaspoon salt
¹/₂ cup warm water,	3¹/₂–4¹/₂ cups
extra	unbleached plain
¹/₂ teaspoon caster	flour
sugar	¹/₄ cup rolled oats, extra

1.～Brush a 12 x 28 cm bread or loaf tin with melted butter or oil; line base with baking paper. Combine oats and water in small pan, stir over low heat 3 minutes or until water is absorbed and oats softened. Place in large bowl; set aside until lukewarm. Dissolve yeast in extra water; add caster sugar. Add yeast, milk, brown sugar and salt to oats; stir well to combine. Add 3¹/₂ cups of flour, 1 cup at a time, until a soft dough forms.
2.～Turn onto a floured surface; knead for

10 minutes, adding remaining flour as necessary, until dough is smooth and elastic. Place dough in large lightly oiled bowl, brush surface with melted butter or oil. Cover with plastic wrap; leave in a warm place 1 hour or until well risen.
3.～Punch down dough and knead for 1 minute. Divide into two; pat out or roll one portion into a rectangle 28 x 18 cm. Roll up loosely and place, seam underneath, into tin. Divide extra dough into 3 pieces; roll each into a sausage

30 cm long. Plait, and then brush with water.
4.～Sprinkle extra oats onto board; turn over plaited dough; press top gently onto oats. Turn and place in tin on other dough, stretching gently to fit snugly. Cover with plastic wrap; leave in a warm place 45 minutes or until risen to top of tin. Preheat oven to 180°C. Bake 45 minutes or until inserted skewer comes out dry. Set aside for 10 minutes; turn onto wire rack to cool. Good with butter and jam.
Note～Keeps well for up to 4 days.

Stir over low heat until water is absorbed and oats are softened.

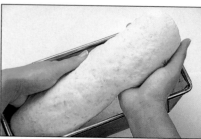

Roll one portion of dough up loosely and place, with seam underneath, in tin.

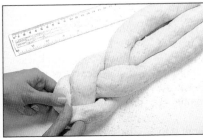

Divide other portion of dough into three long sausage shapes and then plait.

Gently press the plaited dough into the extra rolled oats.

~ Chapatis ~

Preparation time:
40 minutes + standing time
Total cooking time:
40 minutes

Makes 20

2½ cups fine wholemeal flour 1 teaspoon salt 1 tablespoon oil	1 cup warm water ½ cup fine wholemeal flour, extra

1 Place flour and salt in large mixing bowl; make a well in centre. Add oil and water all at once; use a wooden spoon, then hands, to mix to a firm dough.
2 Turn onto lightly floured surface; knead 15 minutes. Do not incorporate the extra flour at this stage. Form into a smooth ball and place in a bowl. Cover with plastic wrap and set aside for at least 2 hours. Can be left overnight, if desired.
3 Divide dough into 20 even-sized pieces. Form each piece into a smooth ball. With the aid of the extra flour, roll each ball into a thin, pancake-size circle. Cover each chapati with floured plastic wrap and leave to rest while rolling remaining dough.
4 Heat a heavy-based frying pan to hot. Cook each chapati 1 minute, turn and cook a further minute. Adjust heat so that dough browns but does not burn. While chapati is cooking, press edges with a folded tea towel. This helps bubbles form and makes the chapati lighter.
5 Wrap and stack in a clean tea towel to keep warm and soft. Serve immediately with curry and vegetable dishes.
Note Roti flour is fine wholemeal flour, and is available from health food shops.

~ Tortillas ~

Preparation time:
1 hour
Total cooking time:
20 minutes

Makes sixteen x 20 cm, twenty x 15 cm or forty x 10 cm tortillas

1½ cups plain flour, sifted	1 cup maize meal, sifted 1 cup warm water

1 Combine flour and maize meal in a large bowl. Make a well in the centre; gradually add warm water. Using a knife, mix to a firm dough. Turn onto lightly floured surface. Knead dough for 3 minutes or until smooth.
2 Divide dough into required portions. Roll out one portion at a time on a lightly floured surface until very thin (about paper thickness). Set aside, cover with plastic wrap; repeat with remaining portions.
3 Heat a dry heavy-based frying pan or flatplate. Place one tortilla in the dry pan.

Chapatis (top) and Tortillas

When the edges begin to curl slightly, turn and cook other side. A few seconds each side is ample cooking time. If residual flour begins to burn in the pan, wipe out with paper towels.

Note ～ Fresh tortillas (pronounced tort-ee-yah) will soften when set aside. Tear into pieces and serve with dips, or roll up with filling for a burrito.

Tortillas will remain fresh for a week in an airtight container. Warm quickly in oven or microwave. Stale tortillas can be torn or cut into bite-size pieces and fried in lard or oil until crisp.

~ Pumpkin Bread ~

Preparation time:
**35 minutes +
2 hours standing**
Total cooking time:
40 minutes

Makes 1 round loaf

7 g sachet dried yeast	**¼–½ cup reserved**
¼ cup reserved warm	**warm pumpkin**
pumpkin cooking	**cooking liquid or**
liquid or water	**water, extra**
4–4½ cups unbleached	**1 egg, beaten**
plain flour	**2 teaspoons water,**
1 teaspoon salt	**extra**
1 cup mashed pumpkin	**pumpkin seeds**
(300 g uncooked)	**(pepitas), to sprinkle**

1 ~ Brush a deep 20 cm cake tin with melted butter or oil; line base with baking paper. Dissolve yeast in reserved pumpkin liquid or water; cover with plastic wrap and leave in a warm place 5 minutes or until frothy. Sift 4 cups of the flour and salt into a large bowl. Add pumpkin, yeast mixture and ¼ cup of the extra liquid. Mix thoroughly using a wooden spoon, then your hands, until well

combined. The dough will form a rough, slightly sticky ball. Add more liquid if mixture is too dry—the amount of liquid will depend on moistness of pumpkin.
2 ~ Turn onto a floured surface. Knead for 10 minutes or until dough is smooth and elastic. Incorporate remaining ½ cup of flour as necessary to form a smooth dough. Place dough into a lightly oiled bowl, brush surface of dough with oil. Cover with plastic wrap and leave in a warm place for 1 hour or until well risen.
3 ~ Punch down dough and knead for 1 minute. Pull away a golf ball-sized piece of dough. Shape the remaining large piece of dough into a smooth round ball and place into prepared tin. Roll smaller ball into a rope 35 cm long. Tie

into a loose knot; place across top of dough and seal with a little water to hold in place. Cover with plastic wrap and leave to rise in a warm place for 1 hour or until well risen to top of tin.
4 ~ Preheat oven to 210°C (Gas 190°C). Brush dough with combined beaten egg and extra water. Sprinkle with pumpkin seeds. Bake 20 minutes, and then reduce oven to 180°C. Bake a further 20 minutes or until cooked. Cover with foil during last 10 minutes of cooking if bread is browning too much. Remove from oven and cool on a wire rack. Pumpkin bread is delicious served just plain with butter
Note ~ Pumpkin bread will keep for up to 3 days in an airtight container, and it also freezes well.

Place knot across top of dough, and then seal with water.

Brush with combined beaten egg and water and sprinkle with pumpkin seeds.

∼ Fruit Bread & Rolls ∼

Dried fruit adds a characteristic sweetness and texture to fruit breads and rolls,
which are a healthy and nutritious alternative to other sweet foods.

Fruit and Nut Bread

Sift 2 1/4 cups plain unbleached white flour into a large bowl. Add a 7 g sachet of dried yeast, 1 teaspoon ground mixed spice, 2 tablespoons caster sugar, 2 teaspoons grated orange rind, 1/3 cup sultanas, 1/4 cup currants, 1 tablespoon mixed peel and 1/4 cup chopped pecans; mix well. Make a well in the centre of flour mixture. Combine 1/3 cup fresh orange juice, 1 egg, 30 g melted butter and 1/3 cup warm water, and add to

flour mixture. Using a wooden spoon, mix to form a soft dough. Turn onto a lightly floured surface; knead for 10 minutes or until the dough is smooth and elastic; add extra flour, if needed. Press with finger to test if done—it will spring back and not leave an indent when ready. Place in a large lightly oiled bowl and brush surface with oil. Cover and leave in a warm place for about 45 minutes or until well risen. Punch down and knead for 1 minute.

Shape into a smooth elongated or round ball. Place ball, if elongated, in a 21 x 11 x 7 cm oiled loaf tin. If round, place on a greased tray and pat out to a 23 cm circle.

Brush surface with oil or melted butter. Cover; leave to rise in warm place for 30 minutes. Bake in a preheated 180°C oven for 20–30 minutes or until cooked. Turn out onto a wire rack. Brush while hot with 1 tablespoon of milk combined with 1 tablespoon sugar. Serve warm or cold.

Fruit and Nut Loaves with a batch of Sticky Bun Scrolls.

Sticky Bun Scrolls

Sift 3 cups of unbleached plain flour, 1/3 cup full cream milk powder, 1/2 teaspoon salt and 1 teaspoon mixed spice into large bowl. Stir in two 7 g sachets dried yeast, and 1/2 cup each caster sugar, currants and sultanas. Make a well in centre of flour mixture. Combine 50 g melted butter, 1 cup warm water and a lightly beaten egg. Add all at once to flour mixture and stir 2–3 minutes until well combined. Add up to 1 cup of flour to make a soft dough.

Turn onto a lightly floured board. Knead for 10 minutes or until the dough is smooth and elastic. Place in large, lightly oiled bowl and brush surface of dough with oil. Cover with plastic wrap. Leave to rise for 1 hour in warm place or until well risen.

Punch down dough; knead 1 minute. Roll to a 30 x 45 cm rectangle. Brush with 30 g melted butter, then sprinkle with 1/2 cup soft brown sugar combined with 1 teaspoon cinnamon. Roll from long side; cut roll into 16 even pieces.

Place on well oiled oven trays, 5 cm apart. Flatten each scroll slightly. Cover with lightly oiled plastic wrap; leave in warm place for 35–40 minutes

or until well risen. Bake in a preheated oven 210°C (190° Gas) for 5 minutes, reduce temperature to 180°C and cook 10 minutes or until cooked. Place on wire rack. Brush several times with 1/3 cup warmed honey. Spread Glacé Icing over scrolls while they are warm.

Glacé Icing: Combine 2 cups icing sugar, 30 g butter and about 1–2 tablespoons milk in a small mixing bowl. Stir until smooth and glossy, and then tint with food colouring.

～ Brioche ～

Preparation time:
**1 hour + 2 ³/₄ hours
standing**
Total cooking time:
1 hour

**Makes 6 small and
1 medium brioche**

---

7 g sachet dried yeast
¹/₂ cup warm milk
1 teaspoon caster
  sugar
4 cups unbleached
  plain flour
1 teaspoon salt
2 tablespoons caster
  sugar, extra
4 eggs, room temper-
  ature, lightly beaten
175 g butter, softened
¹/₄ cup flour, extra,
  for kneading
1 egg yolk, to glaze
1 tablespoon cream

---

1 ～Brush 6 small brioche moulds and a 21 x 11 cm bread or loaf tin with melted butter or oil (see Note). Dissolve yeast in the warm milk, stir in sugar; cover with plastic wrap and leave for 5 minutes or until frothy. In a large bowl, sift flour, salt and extra sugar; make a well in centre. Pour in beaten eggs and yeast mixture.

Using a wooden spoon, beat mixture until it is well combined and forms a rough ball.
2 ～Turn out onto a lightly floured surface; knead for 5 minutes until dough is smooth and firm. Gradually incorporate small amounts of the softened butter into dough. Pull and stretch dough with the aid of a spatula until all the butter is added. This process takes about 10 minutes and dough will be very sticky.
3 ～Clean working surface and hands; sprinkle surface, hands and dough with a small amount of the extra flour. Knead dough lightly 10 minutes or until it is smooth and elastic. Place in a large buttered bowl, brush surface of dough with oil; cover with plastic wrap. Leave in a warm place 1¹/₂–2 hours or until dough is well risen. Punch down dough and divide in half. Cover one half with plastic wrap; set aside. Divide other half into 6 even-sized pieces. Remove a quarter of the dough from each piece. Mould the larger pieces into even rounds and place

into 6 prepared moulds; brush with glaze made of combined egg yolk and cream. Shape small pieces into even rounds, and place in a small ball on top of each roll. Using a floured wooden skewer, push skewer through centre of top ball to the base of the roll; withdraw skewer. This secures the ball to the roll. Brush again with glaze, cover and set aside in a warm place for 45 minutes or until well risen. Preheat oven to 210°C (190°C Gas) and bake brioche for 10 minutes. Reduce oven to 180°C and bake 10 minutes or until golden and cooked. Turn out immediately onto a wire rack to cool.
4 ～Meanwhile place other half of dough into tin, and brush with glaze. Cover and leave to rise 1 hour or until well risen. Bake in 210°C (190°C Gas) oven for 15 minutes; reduce oven to 180°C and cook 15 minutes or until golden and cooked. Turn out immediately onto a wire rack to cool.
Note ～If moulds are not available you may prefer to bake the dough as 2 loaves.

Gradually incorporate small amounts of softened butter into dough.

Push a thick wooden skewer through centre of dough to base.

~ Stollen ~

Preparation time:
45 minutes + 2 hours standing + 2 hours soaking
Total cooking time:
35–40 minutes

Makes 1 oval-shaped loaf

1/2 cup raisins	1/4 cup caster sugar
1/4 cup currants	1 teaspoon grated orange rind
2 tablespoons mixed peel, chopped	3–3 1/2 cups unbleached plain flour
1/4 cup glacé cherries, halved	1/2 teaspoon salt
2 tablespoons rum	1 egg, lightly beaten
7 g sachet dried yeast	1/4 cup slivered almonds
1/3 cup warm water	20 g butter extra, melted
60 g butter	icing sugar, for dusting
1/2 cup milk	

1 Brush a baking tray with melted butter or oil. Combine the raisins, currants, peel and cherries in a bowl, and stir the rum through the mixture. Cover and leave a minimum of 2 hours or until rum is absorbed by the fruit.
2 Dissolve yeast in warm water; cover with plastic wrap and leave in a warm place for 5 minutes or until frothy. Heat butter, milk, sugar and rind in a small pan until mixture is just warm and the butter is melted. Sift 3 cups of the flour and salt into a large

bowl; make a well in the centre. Add yeast, milk mixture and beaten egg. Mix until well combined. Add enough of the remaining flour to make a soft dough.
3 Turn onto a lightly floured surface. Knead for 10 minutes or until dough is smooth and elastic. Place dough into a lightly oiled bowl. Brush surface of dough with melted butter or oil; cover and leave in a warm place for 1 hour or until well risen. Punch down dough and knead for 1 minute. Flatten into a 25 cm square, and then scatter fruit and almonds over the top. Fold dough over fruit and knead fruit lightly into dough until evenly incorporated.
4 Roll dough to an oval shape roughly 30 x 20 cm. Place on baking tray; brush

surface of dough lightly with melted butter. Press rolling pin lengthways across the dough. Fold the dough over the indentation, leaving a 2 cm edge on far side of dough. Brush surface of stollen with melted butter; cover and leave in a warm place for 1 hour or until well risen. Preheat oven to 180°C. Bake for 30–35 minutes or until golden brown. Cool on a wire rack. Dust thickly with icing sugar. Serve cut into thick slices.
Note The shape of this German Christmas bread symbolises the baby Jesus in swaddling clothes. Traditionally, two loaves are baked at the same time—one is for giving and the other is for keeping.
Keeps up to 1 week in an airtight container.

Knead the dried fruit lightly into dough until evenly mixed.

Press rolling pin lengthways down the centre of dough.

～ Finger Buns ～

Preparation time:
**45 minutes + 1 hour
25 minutes standing**
Total cooking time:
12–15 minutes

Makes 12

4 cups unbleached plain
  flour
1/3 cup full cream milk
  powder
2 x 7 g sachets dried
  yeast
1/2 teaspoon salt
1/2 cup caster sugar
1/2 cup sultanas
60 g butter, melted
1 cup warm water

1 egg, lightly beaten
1 egg yolk, extra
1 tablespoon water,
  extra

Glacé Icing
1 1/4 cups icing sugar
20 g butter, melted
2–3 teaspoons water
pink food colouring

1. Brush 2 large oven trays with melted butter or oil. Place 3 cups of the flour, milk powder, yeast, salt, sugar and sultanas in a large bowl and mix well; make a well in the centre. Combine butter, water and egg, and then add all at once to flour. Stir for 2–3 minutes or until well combined. Add enough remaining flour to make a soft dough.

2. Turn out onto a lightly floured surface. Knead 10 minutes or until dough is smooth and elastic. Place dough in a large lightly oiled bowl; brush surface with oil. Cover with plastic wrap and leave to rise in a warm place for 1 hour or until well risen.

3. Punch down dough and knead for 1 minute. Divide dough into 12 even-sized pieces. Shape each piece into a 15 cm-long oval. Place on oven trays 5 cm apart. Cover with plastic wrap and set aside in a warm place for about 20–25 minutes or until well risen.

4. Preheat oven to 180°C. Brush well with combined egg yolk and extra water. Bake for 12–15 minutes or until cooked. Remove and cool on a wire rack.

5. **To make Glacé Icing**: Combine icing sugar, butter and water in a bowl. Stir until smooth. Add colouring, mix well. Use a knife to spread icing over buns.

Note Keeps 2 days, iced, in an airtight container. Freezes, without icing, for up to 1 month.

Place flour, milk powder, yeast, salt, sugar and sultanas in a large bowl.

Divide dough into 12 even-sized pieces and mould each piece into an oval shape.

Brush well with glaze made of egg yolk combined with water.

Using a flat-bladed or palette knife, spread icing over buns.

~ Swedish Tea Ring ~

Preparation time:
**1 hour + 1³/₄ hours
standing**
Total cooking time:
45 minutes

Makes 1 tea ring

7 g sachet dried yeast	**Filling**
2 tablespoons warm water	**30 g butter**
²/₃ cup milk	**1 tablespoon caster sugar**
60 g softened butter	**¹/₂ cup coarsely ground blanched almonds**
2 tablespoons caster sugar	**¹/₂ cup mixed fruit**
¹/₂ teaspoon salt	**¹/₂ cup glacé cherries, halved**
2¹/₂–3 cups unbleached plain flour	
1 egg, lightly beaten	**Icing**
1 egg yolk, extra	**1 cup icing sugar**
1 tablespoon cold water	**1–2 tablespoons milk**
	2 drops almond essence

1 ~ Brush an oven tray with melted butter or oil. Dissolve yeast in warm water. Leave, covered with plastic wrap, for 5 minutes or until bubbles appear on surface. Heat milk, butter, sugar and salt in a pan until just warmed. Sift 2 cups of the flour into a large bowl. Add the yeast and milk mixtures and beaten egg. Mix thoroughly until a smooth batter is formed. Add enough of the remaining flour to make a soft dough. Turn out onto a lightly floured surface. Knead for 10 minutes or until the dough is smooth and elastic. Place dough in a large, lightly oiled bowl and brush surface of dough with oil. Cover with plastic wrap; leave in warm place for 1 hour or until well risen.

2 ~ **To make Filling:** Cream butter and caster sugar; combine with almonds, mixed fruit and cherries.

3 ~ Punch dough down, and then knead for 1 minute. Roll dough to a 25 cm x 45 cm rectangle. Spread filling over dough to within 2 cm of border. Roll up dough; form into a ring with seam underneath roll. Seal ends together with a little combined egg yolk and water. Place on the prepared oven tray.

4 ~ Snip with scissors from outside edge every 4 cm. Turn cut pieces on side and flatten slightly. Cover with plastic wrap; leave in a warm place for 45 minutes or until well risen. Brush dough with combined egg yolk and cold water.

Bake in preheated 180°C oven for 20–25 minutes or until cooked. Cover with foil if browning too much. Remove and cool. Serve this sweet loaf for morning or afternoon tea.

5 ~ **To make Icing:** Combine ingredients until smooth. Drizzle icing over tea ring. Accompany with extra cherries, if desired.

Note ~ Keeps 3 days in an airtight container. Freezes, without icing, for up to 1 month.

Roll up dough after spreading filling over top to within about 2 cm of edge.

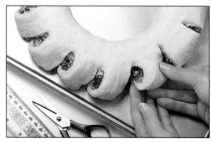

Turn the cut pieces on their sides and flatten them slightly.

～ Sally Lunn ～

Preparation time:
**35 minutes + 2¹/₂ hours
standing**
Total cooking time:
45 minutes

Makes 1 bun

7 g sachet dried yeast	125 g butter, melted
¹/₄ cup warm water	¹/₂ teaspoon salt
1 teaspoon caster sugar	4 cups unbleached plain flour
3 eggs, at room temperature	1 tablespoon sugar, extra
³/₄ cup warm milk	1 tablespoon milk, extra
¹/₃ cup honey	

1～Brush a deep 25 cm round tin with melted butter or oil and line the base with baking paper. Dissolve the yeast in warm water and add sugar. Cover with plastic wrap; leave in a warm place for 5 minutes or until frothy. Place the eggs, milk, honey, butter, salt, 2 cups of the flour and the yeast mixture in the large bowl of an electric mixer. Beat at medium speed for 5 minutes. Remove from mixer and stir in enough of the remaining flour to make a thick batter.

2～Cover loosely with plastic wrap. Leave to rise in a warm place 1–1¹/₂ hours or until well risen. Stir down the batter.
3～Using a ladle or spoon, place the batter in the prepared tin. Flatten the surface of the batter with lightly oiled hands. Cover and leave to rise again for 1 hour or until batter reaches the top of the tin.
4～Preheat oven to 180°C. Bake for 35–40 minutes or until a skewer inserted in the centre comes out clean. Brush with combined

extra sugar and milk and return to the oven for 5 minutes. Turn out onto a cake rack and set aside for 20 minutes. Slice and serve while still warm.
Note～You may like to try the traditional serving method. To do this, leave bread to cool, and then slice it into 3 equal layers. Toast and butter each side, then reassemble into the original bun shape. Slice and serve. This English cake-like bread is often served for afternoon tea. Keeps for up to 5 days in an airtight container. Freezes for 1 month.

Stir in enough of the remaining flour to make a thick batter.

Leave dough to stand in a warm place until it is well risen.

Using a ladle, place the dough in the prepared tin.

Brush the top of the cooked bread with the combined sugar and milk.

~ Challah ~

Preparation time:
50 minutes + 1³/₄ hours standing
Total cooking time:
40 minutes

Makes 2 medium braided loaves

2 x 7 g sachets dried
  yeast
¹/₂ cup warm water
6 cups unbleached plain
  flour
1 teaspoon salt
1 tablespoon caster
  sugar

60 g butter, melted
2 eggs, lightly beaten
1 cup warm water,
  extra
1 egg yolk
2 teaspoons water
sesame seeds

1 Brush a large baking tray with melted butter or oil. Dissolve yeast in warm water. Sift 4 cups of the flour, salt and sugar into a large bowl. Make a well in the centre and pour in butter, beaten eggs and dissolved yeast. Cover mixture with a little of the flour, cover with plastic wrap and set aside 10 minutes or until yeast is frothy. Add extra water and stir mixture until well incorporated. Beat with a wooden spoon for 5 minutes. Add enough of the remaining flour to make a soft dough.
2 Turn out onto a lightly floured surface and knead 10 minutes or until dough is smooth and elastic. Place dough in a lightly oiled bowl; brush surface of dough with melted butter or oil. Cover and leave in a warm place for 1 hour or until well risen. Punch down dough and knead for 1 minute. Divide dough into 2 equal halves. Return one half to bowl, cover with plastic wrap; leave to rise again while preparing first challah.
3 Divide remaining half into 3 equal pieces. Roll pieces into ropes about 3 cm thick and 30 cm long. Place ropes side by side on tray and plait from centre. Pinch ends and tuck under to seal. Cover and leave to rise 45 minutes or until well risen. Punch down other half of dough and shape as above. Leave to rise while the first challah is cooking.
4 Preheat oven to 180°C. Brush first challah with combined egg yolk and water and sprinkle with sesame seeds. Bake for 35–40 minutes or until bread is golden brown and sounds hollow when tapped. Cool on a wire rack. Bake the second challah and cool.
Note This Jewish bread, pronounced 'hallah', is traditionally baked in 2 loaves for the Sabbath evening meal. It may also be made as one very large challah, if preferred.

Keeps for up to 4 days in an airtight container or freezes well for up to 1 month.

Place the dough ropes side by side on a baking tray and then plait.

Brush with combined egg yolk and water and sprinkle with sesame seeds.

~ Cream Buns ~

Preparation time:
30 minutes + 1¹⁄₄ hours standing
Total cooking time:
20 minutes

Makes 12

3¹⁄₂ cups plain flour, sifted	7 g sachet dried yeast
2 tablespoons sugar	1¹⁄₄ cups cream
¹⁄₂ teaspoon salt	1 tablespoon icing sugar
1¹⁄₃ cups milk, warmed	¹⁄₂ cup raspberry or strawberry jam
60 g butter, melted	2 tablespoons icing sugar, extra

1 ~ Brush two oven trays with melted butter or oil. Dust trays lightly with flour; shake off any excess. Place half the flour, half the sugar and half the salt in a food processor. Combine milk and butter in a small bowl, sprinkle with the yeast; stir to dissolve. Pour half the yeast mixture onto ingredients in processor. Process for 30 seconds until a soft, smooth dough forms. Transfer to lightly oiled bowl. Repeat procedure with remaining flour and yeast mixtures; combine with first dough in oiled bowl. Set aside, covered with plastic wrap, in a warm place for 1 hour or until well risen.

2 ~ Punch down dough and turn onto lightly floured surface; knead for 2 minutes or until smooth. Divide into 12 pieces. Knead one portion at a time for 30 seconds on a lightly floured surface, and then shape into a ball.

3 ~ Preheat oven to 210°C (190°C Gas). Place balls of dough, evenly spaced, onto prepared trays. Set aside, covered with plastic wrap, in a warm place for 15 minutes or until

well risen. Bake for 20 minutes or until well browned and cooked through. Set aside for 5 minutes; transfer to a wire rack to cool. Using a serrated knife, cut diagonally into each bun, to a depth of 5 cm, from the top of bun towards the base.

4 ~ Using electric beaters, beat cream and sugar in a small bowl until firm peaks form. Fill the buns with piped whipped cream and jam. Dust with icing sugar.

Note ~ If a large food processor is available, process flour and yeast mixtures in one step.

Dust oiled tray lightly with flour, and then shake off any excess.

Process in food processor until a soft, smooth dough forms.

Place balls, evenly spaced, onto the prepared tray.

Using a serrated knife, make a diagonal cut in each cooked bun.

~ Greek Easter Bread ~

Preparation time:
2 hours 10 minutes
Total cooking time:
**40 minutes + 1 hour 40
minutes standing**

Makes 1 loaf

7 g sachet dried yeast	1 teaspoon ground anise
2 tablespoons warm water	1 egg, lightly beaten
1/2 cup milk	
60 g butter	*Topping*
1/2 teaspoon salt	1 egg, lightly beaten
1/4 cup caster sugar	1 tablespoon milk
1 teaspoon grated orange rind	1 tablespoon each sesame seeds, chopped slivered almonds and caster sugar
2 1/2 –3 cups unbleached plain flour	

1.~Brush an oven tray with melted butter or oil. Dissolve yeast in warm water and set aside for 5 minutes or until frothy. Combine milk, butter, salt, sugar and orange rind in a small pan. Heat until butter has melted and milk is just warm. Sift 2 1/2 cups of the flour and the anise into a large bowl. Make a well in the centre, add yeast, milk mixture and egg. Gradually beat into flour for 1 minute or until a smooth dough forms.

2.~Turn out onto a lightly floured surface. Knead for 10 minutes, incorporating remaining

flour, until dough is smooth and elastic. Return to lightly oiled bowl and brush surface of dough with melted butter or oil. Cover and set aside in a warm place for 1 hour or until well risen.

3.~Punch down dough, and then knead for 1 minute. Divide dough into 3 equal pieces. Roll each portion into 3 equal strands 35 cm long. Plait the strands and fold ends under. Place on oven tray, brush with the combined beaten egg and milk; sprinkle with sesame seeds, almonds and sugar (if using dyed eggs, add them at this stage—see Note). Cover with lightly oiled plastic wrap; leave in a warm place for 40 minutes or until well risen.

4.~Preheat oven to 180°C. Bake bread for

30–40 minutes or until cooked. It should sound hollow when tapped on the base with knuckles. Serve warm.

Note.~This braided, anise flavoured bread originated in Greece where traditionally it is served at Easter with dyed red eggs nestled snugly into the plaited top. It also looks most attractive without the eggs and is delicious made either way.

Try decorating the bread at Easter time with dyed hard-boiled eggs. Use 1–2 hen eggs or 3–4 quail eggs, and Greek red food dye to colour. Push dyed eggs onto dough after plaiting and before final rising.

Red dye is available in some Greek specialty food stores, and comes with detailed instructions on how to dye eggs.

Sprinkle plaited dough with sesame seeds, almonds and sugar.

If using red eggs, push them into dough after plaiting and before final rising.

～ Chelsea Buns ～

Preparation time:
25 minutes + 1 1/2 hours standing
Total cooking time:
25 minutes

Makes 24

7 g sachet dried yeast	60 g butter, extra
1 teaspoon sugar	1/4 cup soft brown sugar
1 tablespoon plain flour	1 cup mixed dried fruit
1/2 cup milk, warmed	1/2 teaspoon mixed spice, extra
2 1/2 cups plain flour, sifted, extra	
125 g butter, chopped	*Glaze*
1 tablespoon sugar, extra	1 tablespoon milk
1/2 teaspoon mixed spice	2 tablespoons sugar
1 egg, lightly beaten	*Glacé Icing*
2 teaspoons grated lemon rind	1/2 cup icing sugar
	1–2 tablespoons milk

1. ～ Brush a large baking tray with melted butter or oil. Combine yeast, sugar and flour in a small bowl. Gradually add milk and blend until smooth. Set aside, covered with plastic wrap, in a warm place for 5 minutes or until foamy. Place extra flour, butter, sugar and spice in food processor. Process for 30 seconds until mixture is fine and crumbly. Add egg, rind and yeast mixture and process for 15 seconds or until mixture almost forms a dough.

2. ～ Turn onto a lightly floured surface and knead for 2 minutes or until dough is smooth; shape into a ball. Place in a large, lightly oiled bowl; set aside, covered with plastic wrap, in a warm place for 1 hour until dough is well risen. Punch down dough; knead for 2 minutes or until smooth.

3. ～ Preheat oven to 210°C (Gas 190°C). Using electric beaters, beat extra butter and brown sugar in a small bowl until light and creamy. Roll dough out to 40 x 25 cm rectangle. Spread butter and sugar all over the dough to within 2 cm of the edge of one of the longer sides. Spread with the combined fruit and extra spice. Roll dough lengthways, firmly and evenly into a log, Swiss roll-style. This will enclose the fruit and butter mixture. Use a sharp knife to cut the roll into eight slices about 5 cm in width. Arrange the slices, evenly spaced and close together, on the prepared tray. Place the seams inwards and flatten the pieces slightly. Set aside, covered with plastic wrap, in a warm place for 30 minutes or until well risen.

4. ～ Bake buns in preheated oven for 20 minutes or until they are well browned and cooked through. Remove from the oven and brush liberally with the glaze. Transfer to wire rack to cool.

To make Glaze:
Combine milk and sugar in a small pan. Stir over low heat until the sugar dissolves and mixture is almost boiling. Remove from the heat.

To make Glacé Icing:
Combine icing sugar and milk and stir until smooth. Drizzle over the glazed and cooled buns.

Spread butter and sugar over the dough to within about 2 cm of edge.

Arrange slices close together with seams facing inward.

～ Monkey Bread ～

Preparation time:
**30 minutes + 2 hours
standing**
Total cooking time:
45 minutes

Makes 1 loaf

2 x 7 g sachets dried yeast	**4–5 cups unbleached plain flour**
1/2 **cup warm water**	1/2 **teaspoon salt**
1 cup milk	**1 egg, lightly beaten**
60 g butter	**125 g butter, melted**
1/2 **cup caster sugar**	1/2 **cup soft brown sugar**
	1/2 **cup currants**

1～Brush a large tube or angel food tin with melted butter or oil. Dissolve yeast in the warm water, cover with plastic wrap, and leave in a warm place for 5 minutes or until frothy. Heat the milk, butter and sugar in a small pan until butter is melted and the milk is just warm. Sift 4 cups of the flour and salt into a large bowl. Make a well in the centre. Add yeast, milk mixture and egg and mix thoroughly until well combined. Add enough of the remaining flour to make a soft dough.

2～Turn onto a lightly floured surface. Knead 10 minutes or until dough is smooth and elastic; place in a lightly oiled bowl. Brush surface of dough with melted butter or oil, cover with plastic wrap, and leave in a warm place for 1 hour or until well risen.

3～Punch down dough and knead 1 minute. Pull golf ball sized pieces from the dough. Shape each ball into a smooth round. Combine melted butter with brown sugar and currants to make a glaze. Using a metal spoon, dip each ball into the glaze and coat.

4～Arrange the balls in two layers in the prepared tube pan. Cover with plastic wrap; set aside to rise in a warm place for 1 hour or until dough has reached top of pan. Preheat oven to 210°C (190°Gas) and bake for 10 minutes. Reduce oven to 180°C and cook a further 30–35 minutes or until cooked. Leave for 10 minutes in the tin, and then turn out onto a wire rack. Replace tin carefully over the cake and leave to cool. This will ensure that the pieces of bread stay intact. Serve inverted side up and slice or pull apart with hands. Serve this sweet bread with butter for morning or afternoon tea.

Note～To obtain the authentic Monkey Bread shape it is necessary to use a deep pan such as a tube pan or an angel food tin. These tins are usually readily available from specialty kitchenware shops.

This is a popular North American bread, although the origin of the name is not clear— perhaps it relates to the bread's unusual shape

Keeps for up to 5 days in an airtight container or freezes well for up to1 month.

Using a metal spoon, dip each ball into the prepared glaze and coat.

Arrange balls in two layers in prepared tube pan.

～ Kringle ～

Preparation time:
**45 minutes +
30 minutes standing**
Total cooking time:
30 minutes

Makes 1 loaf

60 g softened butter
2–2¹/2 cups unbleached
  plain flour
7 g sachet dried
  yeast
¹/4 cup warm water
2 tablespoons caster
  sugar
¹/4 teaspoon salt
¹/3 cup cream,
  warmed

1 egg, lightly beaten
1 egg extra, separated
1 teaspoon water, extra
2 tablespoons flaked
  almonds
caster sugar, to sprinkle

Filling
¹/2 cup soft brown sugar
¹/2 cup chopped walnuts
1 cup chopped dates

1. ～Brush an oven tray with melted butter or oil. Combine butter and 2 tablespoons of the flour in a small bowl until blended. Use a spatula to spread mixture onto a sheet of waxed paper to 10 x 20 cm. Cover and chill.

2. ～Dissolve yeast in warm water. Cover with plastic wrap; set aside 5 minutes or until frothy. In a large bowl, combine 1 cup of the flour, sugar, salt, cream, egg and yeast mixture; beat until well combined. Add enough of remaining flour to make a soft dough. Turn onto a lightly floured board and knead for 10 minutes or until dough is smooth and elastic. Roll into a 20 cm square. Lift waxed paper with chilled butter mixture and turn over onto dough so that the butter lies down centre of dough; remove waxed paper. Fold one side of dough over butter, then fold other side over to meet in the centre; pinch to seal. Roll into a 15 x 30 cm rectangle. Fold top third of pastry down towards you, and then fold the bottom third up over the top. You should end up with 3 layers of pastry. Turn the pastry clockwise until the open long seam is on the right; press ends together. Roll and fold 3 more times. If dough becomes too soft, refrigerate until firm, and then continue.

3. ～ **To make Filling:** Mix sugar, walnuts and dates to make a filling. Roll dough into a 15 x 70 cm rectangle. Spread the filling down centre of dough. Roll up into a sausage shape, with seam underneath. Brush edges and ends with extra egg yolk to seal.

4. ～Place on prepared oven tray. Shape into a kringle by bringing the two ends round and up to meet in the centre to look like a large capital 'B'. Seal with egg yolk. Cover and set aside to rise for 30 minutes or until well risen. Preheat oven to 180°C. Brush dough with combined beaten egg white and water; sprinkle with almonds and sugar. Bake for 25–30 minutes or until cooked. Turn out and cool on a wire rack.
Note ～The bakers of Scandinavia hang a gilded image of this famous coffee bread outside their shops as a symbol of their trade.

Kringle is also sometimes made in a large horseshoe shape.

Keeps for up to 5 days in an airtight container, and freezes well for up to 1 month.

Spread the filling down the centre of rolled-out dough.

Bring the two ends round and up to meet in the centre in the shape of a capital 'B'.

~ Whole Fruit Bread ~

Preparation time:
**40 minutes + 2 hours
standing**
Total cooking time:
45 minutes

Makes 1 loaf

3½ cups unbleached
  plain flour
1 cup unbleached plain
  wholemeal flour
2 tablespoons caster
  sugar
½ teaspoon salt
7 g sachet dried yeast
1 tablespoon grated
  orange rind
1 cup freshly squeezed
  orange juice

½ cup hot water
2 tablespoons oil
1½ cups mixed whole
  dried fruit, such as
  apricots, dates, figs
  and prunes
½ cup raisins or
  muscatels
1 tablespoon milk,
  warmed
1 tablespoon caster
  sugar, extra

1 Brush a 12 x 11 x 27 cm bread loaf tin with melted butter or oil. Line base with baking paper. Place 3 cups of the plain flour, the wholemeal flour, sugar, salt and yeast in a large bowl; make a well in centre. Combine the orange rind, orange juice, water and oil. Add all at once to flour mixture and stir 2–3 minutes or until well combined. Add enough of the remaining flour to make a soft dough.
2 Turn out onto a lightly floured surface. Knead 10 minutes or until dough is smooth and elastic. Place dough in a large, lightly oiled bowl and lightly oil the surface of the dough. Cover with plastic wrap and set aside in a warm place for 1 hour or until the dough is well risen.
3 Punch down dough, and then pat out to a large plate size. Mix dried fruit with raisins or muscatels; dot half the fruit over top of dough. Carefully fold over the dough and incorporate the fruit, taking care not to squash fruit. Repeat process with remaining fruit, folding dough until fruit is spread through it evenly. The fruit should remain whole during the kneading process.
4 Divide dough into 2 equal portions and form into 2 smooth, slightly elongated balls. Place in prepared tin. Cover with plastic wrap and set aside in a warm place for 1 hour or until dough has risen above top of tin. Preheat oven to 210°C (Gas 190°C). Bake for 10 minutes. Reduce oven to 180°C and bake for a further 30 minutes or until cooked. Cover with foil if loaf is browning too much. Remove from oven; brush loaf top with combined warm milk and sugar, return to oven for 5 minutes. Brush again with milk and sugar glaze, remove from tin and cool on a wire rack. Serve with butter as a healthy snack, or for morning or afternoon tea.
Note May also be served with cheese.

Fold the dough over the fruit and mix together, taking care not to squash fruit.

Place the smooth, slightly elongated balls into the prepared tin.

～ Malt Bread ～

Preparation time:
**45 minutes + 1 hour
40 minutes standing**
Total cooking time:
40 minutes

Makes 1 loaf

1 cup lukewarm water	½ cup raisins
7 g sachet dried yeast	30 g butter, melted
1 teaspoon sugar	1 tablespoon treacle
2 cups plain wholemeal flour	1 tablespoon liquid malt extract
1 cup plain flour	1 tablespoon hot milk
2 teaspoons ground cinnamon	½ teaspoon liquid malt, extra

1 ～ Brush 21 x 14 x 7 cm loaf tin with oil, and then line the base with baking paper. Combine water, yeast and sugar in small mixing bowl. Cover with plastic wrap and set aside in a warm position for 10 minutes or until mixture is foamy. Sift flours and cinnamon into a large bowl; add raisins and stir to combine. Make a well in the centre of mixture. Add melted butter, treacle, malt and yeast mixture.
2 ～ Using a knife, mix to a soft dough. Turn onto a lightly floured surface and knead for 10 minutes or until smooth. Shape dough into a ball and place in a lightly oiled mixing bowl. Set aside, covered with plastic wrap, in a warm place for 1 hour or until well risen. Punch down dough. Knead for 3 minutes or until smooth.
3 ～ Roll dough into a 20 x 20 cm square; roll up with the seam side underneath. Place in tin and set aside, covered with plastic wrap, in a warm place for 40 minutes or until well risen.

4 ～ Preheat oven to 180°C. Brush dough with combined milk and extra malt. Bake for 40 minutes or until well browned and cooked through. Set aside for 3 minutes in tin before transferring to a wire rack to cool.

Sift cinnamon, wholemeal and plain flours into a large bowl.

Using a knife, mix flour and raisin mixture to a soft dough.

Roll up dough square, making sure that the seam is underneath.

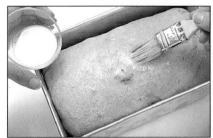

Brush the risen dough with combined hot milk and malt.

～ Index ～

*Front cover, from top
left to bottom: Potato
Bread (p. 18), Grissini
(p. 26), Challah (p. 48),
Cream Buns (p. 50),
Swedish Tea Ring
(p. 44), Brioche (p. 38).*